M366 Block 6
UNDERGRADUATE COMPUTING

Natural and artificial intelligence

Reflections

Block

6

Cover image: Daniel H. Janzen. *Polistes* wasps build a relatively simple nest that lasts only a single summer. These New World wasps often site the unenclosed combs under eaves and the other sheltered places where they come into contact with people.

This publication forms part of an Open University course M366 *Natural and artificial intelligence.* Details of this and other Open University courses can be obtained from the Student Registration and Enquiry Service, The Open University, PO Box 197, Milton Keynes MK7 6BJ, United Kingdom: tel. +44 (0)845 300 6090, email general-enquiries@open.ac.uk

Alternatively, you may visit the Open University website at http://www.open.ac.uk where you can learn more about the wide range of courses and packs offered at all levels by The Open University.

To purchase a selection of Open University course materials visit http://www.ouw.co.uk, or contact Open University Worldwide, Michael Young Building, Walton Hall, Milton Keynes MK7 6AA, United Kingdom for a brochure. tel. +44 (0)1908 858793; fax +44 (0)1908 858787; email ouw-customer-services@open.ac.uk

The Open University
Walton Hall, Milton Keynes
MK7 6AA

First published 2007

Edited and designed by The Open University.

Typeset by SR Nova Pvt. Ltd, Bangalore, India.

Printed and bound in the United Kingdom by The Charlesworth Group, Wakefield.

ISBN 978 0 7492 1583 5

1.1

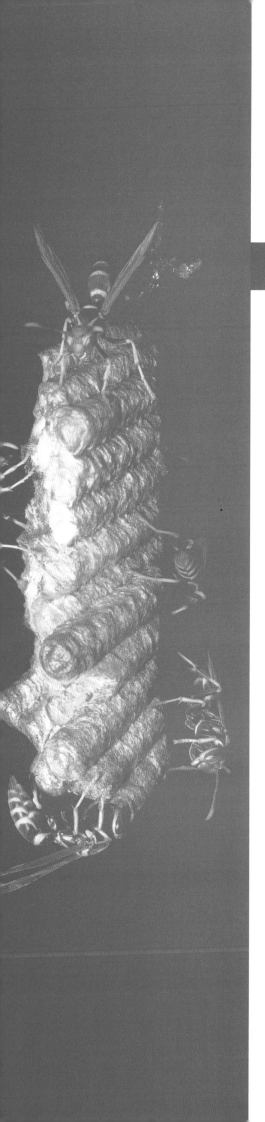

Block 6
Reflections

Prepared for the course team by Syed Mustafa Ali and Chris Dobbyn

CONTENTS

M366 COURSE TEAM

Chair, author and academic editor
Chris Dobbyn

Authors
Mustafa Ali

Tony Hirst

Mike Richards

Neil Smith

Patrick Wong

External assessor
Nigel Crook, Oxford Brookes University

Course managers
Gaynor Arrowsmith

Linda Landsberg

Media development staff
Andrew Seddon, Media Project Manager

Garry Hammond, Editor

Kate Gentles, Freelance Editor

Callum Lester, Software Developer

Andrew Whitehead, Designer and Graphic Artist

Phillip Howe, Compositor

Sarah Gamman, Contracts Executive

Lydia Eaton, Media Assistant

Critical readers
Frances Chetwynd

John Dyke

Ian Kenny

Paolo Remagnino

Thanks are due to the Desktop Publishing Unit of the Faculty of Mathematics and Computing.

Introduction to Block 6

Block introduction

Like Block 1, Block 6 consists of a single unit. Its purpose is to bring down the curtain on M366 in two ways: by speculating about the future of biologically inspired computing, and by looking back over the ground you've covered in the course with the central aim of artificial intelligence (AI) in mind.

In the first section of the unit, I list a few further areas of computing in which biological principles are being applied to computational systems, all of them in the early research stages. These represent what I believe will be a future trend: a further blurring of the boundaries between computers and living systems.

The block ends with a return to some of the questions posed in Block 1. In particular, I address the issue of whether it is possible that machines are, or might become, intelligent in the 'strong' sense. Despite fifty or more years of debate on this subject, you will learn that any consensus on this question is as far away as it was in Alan Turing's time. Nevertheless, I present what I believe are the main arguments. You will want to make up your own minds.

Block 6 learning outcomes

After studying this block you will be able to:

▶ suggest some future directions that biologically inspired AI might take;

▶ describe in a series of bullet points the Chinese Room Argument;

▶ write a paragraph explaining the terms *embodiment*, *situatedness* and *embeddedness*, explaining their potential significance for intelligence;

▶ write a short critical and reflective essay setting out your own views on the possibility of strong AI in machines.

Unit 1: Intelligence, mind and consciousness

CONTENTS

Introduction to Unit 1

In this final block of M366 I have two aims.

Firstly, I want to take a peep into the future and speculate a little on possible developments in biologically inspired computing and AI. I believe that at the start of the twenty-first century, computing research has reached a crucially interesting stage, and that biologically inspired computation may play an increasing role in the future development of the field. I will look briefly at some of these possible futures and offer you pointers towards further reading about them.

Secondly, I want to tie things up by returning to the original objective of the course, and revisiting some of the issues raised in Block 1. Remember that the aim of AI is to *create intelligent machines*. So we now need to consider a few simple questions:

▶ To what extent, if any, could the kinds of systems I've presented in M366 be said to be intelligent?

▶ If so, intelligent in what sense?

▶ Is it possible to create intelligent machines at all?

▶ Does the biologically inspired approach take us any further than conventional symbolic strategies?

Unfortunately, as you will see, simple questions rarely have simple answers.

All I can hope to do in the first section is present a brief review, with pointers for you to follow up any areas you may be interested in. The nature of the material presented in the second part of the block is rather different to that of earlier blocks. It is generally philosophical in nature and takes the form of reflections on how some of the classic arguments directed at Symbolic AI may apply to biologically inspired AI.

What you need to study this unit

You will need the following course components, and will need to use your computer and internet connection for some of the exercises.

▶ this Block 6 text

▶ the course DVD.

LEARNING OUTCOMES FOR UNIT 1

After studying this unit you will be able to:

1.1 define the terms 'strong' and 'weak' in the context of biologically inspired AI;

1.2 explain the difference between symbolic and sub-symbolic AI;

1.3 describe the Chinese Room Argument and the main responses to this thought experiment;

1.4 list the main characteristics of artificial life (A-Life) and briefly explain the argument for A-Life as a route to AI;

1.5 explain what is meant by embodiment, situatedness and embeddedness and their relation to biologically inspired AI;

1.6 describe the 'hard problem' of consciousness and explain its possible relevance to the debate over strong AI;

1.7 describe the basic features of computational life and living computers.

2 What now? The future of biologically inspired computing

In this section, I want to speculate for a moment on the possible future of biologically inspired computing. Most visions of the future look preposterous by the time the future actually arrives. Twentieth-century science-fiction films representing twenty-first century men and women clad in Lycra catsuits, racing through megacities in jetcars, seem quaint today. And most predictions of future technologies fall flat on their faces. The popular BBC television programme *Tomorrow's World* brought us the fold-up car and the solar-powered, air-conditioned hat, but failed to foresee the rise of the personal computer. So we have to be cautious. How might the field develop?

Three quests, among others, motivated the development of computer technologies in the last century: for smaller size, for greater speed and for increased reliability. The computer pioneer John von Neumann expected that with increasing complexity of computer hardware there would have to be major advances in the theory of computation. These have not occurred. But as early as 1948, von Neumann had observed that:

> Natural organisms are, as a rule, much more complicated and subtle, and therefore much less well understood in detail, than are artificial automata. Nevertheless, some regularities which we observe in the organization of the former may be quite instructive in our thinking and planning of the latter.

Source: von Neumann, J. (1948), Hixon Lecture

Hardware and software engineers look with envy at living systems. Although the miniaturisation of electronic circuits has been an astounding success story, nature tends to work at higher speeds and on atomic or molecular scales of size. Whereas computer hardware is fragile, and software generally unreliable, biological systems are fault tolerant and self-repairing. Moreover, whereas it takes costly engineering efforts to build computer hardware and software, living systems *self-assemble*, growing from a single cell to massive complexity, in a process known as **morphogenesis**.

One prospect seems fairly likely: a further blurring of the boundaries between computers and living systems. The examples that follow are all very brief accounts of a few of the ways in which computing researchers are taking up the challenge of mimicking some of these remarkable powers of nature – in computers that imitate life, and in living computers.

2.1 Computational life

Amorphous computing

The robustness of living systems is partly based on a simple principle: massive redundancy. If a single cell dies or malfunctions, there are millions of others to bear the burden.

The MIT Artificial Intelligence Laboratory has become a leader in the field of research known as **amorphous computing**. Amorphous computing attempts to exploit the fact that very tiny microprocessors can today be produced in their millions at very little cost. If, instead of building a system around a single chip, one could instead use thousands of minute, cheap microprocessors, there would be no problem if many of them malfunctioned. Such a system, in the words of one of the laboratory's most prominent researchers, Gerry Sussman, could be made to act as 'a co-operating combination of redundant systems'.

MIT scientists have experimented with a number of such systems, and attempted to establish some of the theoretical principles on which they could compute. One idea is to embed at random thousands of tiny micro-processors, capable of signalling to one another and to the outside world by (very short range) wireless, into some substrate, such as a paint or gel. If one of these processors proves defective, or breaks down, then the others will simply ignore it. Such a material could then, they suggest, be painted onto structures such as bridges. In place, they could report on factors such as cracks, stress factors and loads, and might even be able to repair minor damage if the microprocessors were equipped with actuators.

Other groups have developed fault-tolerant self-repairing computers out of massive arrays of chips. The Teramac computer, developed by Hewlett-Packard, for example, uses over seven million simple chips. In trials, it was able to self-fix over 200 000 faults and continue to compute as well as top-of-the-range HP workstations, even despite the fact that at least 3% of its chips were faulty. There has also been research into amorphous software, such as the Growing Point Language (also developed at MIT), in which programs can be written to govern the self-organised growth of amorphous hardware.

I've provided a number of web links to sites devoted to amorphous computing on the course website and/or the course DVD. You may explore these at your leisure.

Self-developing hardware

Today, microprocessors are produced according to rigorous engineering principles: a design is drawn up and finalised; a production system is set up and tested; and then the chips are produced and tested in their millions. Defective chips simply have to be thrown away. Once produced, the circuitry cannot be changed, so the original design has to be quite general purpose, in order that the hardware can be deployed in different contexts, which are always liable to change.

This is not nature's way. Living 'machines' are not designed: they grow and evolve. And they are general purpose in a quite different way to modern electronic circuits, in that they continually adapt themselves to changing circumstances. Defective individuals are capable of a limited amount of self-repair. Systems that somehow grow and evolve in ways similar to living organisms are broadly known as **POEtic** machines. Developing such machines is, of course, a massive challenge. Current research efforts are almost all in the field of evolvable and self-growing electronic circuitry. There are two main approaches: to mimic either evolution or morphogenesis.

Evolutionary hardware

After having worked through Block 5, you're now well aware of software techniques based on genetic algorithms (GAs). The most straightforward approach to evolvable hardware, then, is to work with reconfigurable chips and to evolve these using a GA.

Reconfigurable chips have been available since the 1980s in the shape of **field-programmable gate arrays** (**FPGAs**). FPGAs are made up of clusters of interconnected logic units that are fully reconfigurable: that is, it is possible to alter the logic of units, the interconnections between them and the nature of the inputs and outputs they receive. Changes to the chip are made on nanosecond timescales. Since it is easy to completely specify the desired architecture of an FPGA as a bit string, it is obviously possible to devise systems that combine these devices with a GA to evolve circuits that can respond to a changing environment and to completely novel problems.

Researchers see applications of evolvable hardware in communications technology, electro-photographic printing and data compression. The ultimate challenge is to take the evolutionary process out of software altogether, and for all evolution to take place on the chip itself. However, this is a distant prospect.

Embryonic hardware

The development of an organism starts with a single cell. From this, the entire creature, in all its complexity, grows. As I said earlier, this process is known as *morphogenesis*. Exactly how something as complex as a human being can arise from a sparse genetic plan is still largely mysterious.

Attempts at producing morphogenetic microprocessors are still in their early infancy. A research group at The Swiss Federal Institute of Technology have developed a small embryonic system, the Biowatch, on genetic and morphogenetic principles. There are links to this project, and other bio-inspired hardware groups, on the course website and/or the course DVD.

Immune system computing

No one who owns a networked computer can be unaware of the constant danger of cyber-attack. Our machines are under permanent and relentless attack from viruses, Trojans, malware, 'phishing', etc. Millions of pounds are wasted every year in lost productivity and computer fraud, and a vast security industry has grown up in response to the problem.

Living bodies are under perpetual attack too, principally from viruses and bacteria; and the bodies of higher animals have evolved sophisticated defences against these, known as **immune systems**. As with all good defensive systems, the bodies of mammals are protected by defences layered in depth. There are four levels at which the mammalian body is prepared to repel or destroy **pathogens**:

▶ the skin and mucous membranes – these present a formidable barrier to invading organisms;

▶ a hot and acidic internal environment damages and can be fatal to organisms that make it through the skin;

▶ the **innate immune system**, consisting mainly of the white blood cells, which circulate around the body destroying pathogens;

▶ the **adaptive immune system**, which recognises new pathogens and manufactures killer T and B cells specifically for use against them. This form of 'learning' seems to be Darwinian in nature, with millions of different types of killer cells perpetually being developed, and the effective ones selected.

The crucial ability of the immune system is to distinguish between 'self' and 'non-self': to recognise and tolerate cells that belong to the organism itself and to attack all non-self particles. Diseases like lupus are the result of the immune system ceasing to be able to make this key distinction.

One key research challenge, then, is to build computer security systems on the model of the mammalian immune system. You can see that the robustness and fault tolerance of the biological immune system again arises from massive redundancy, and also from its distributed nature: it is not located in any single site in the body, but throughout it. It also has a number of powerful properties that an artificial immune system (AIS) should try to duplicate:

▶ *defence in depth* – ideally an AIS should consist of a number of diverse layers of defence;

▶ *autonomy* – an AIS should work in the background, independently of user control;

▶ *flexibility* – an AIS should be able to respond automatically to new kinds of threat, to *learn* the right defences to them and to *remember* what it has learned.

Research is underway in a number of laboratories around the world. Most of this is into AIS-like software systems, but there is some very early work investigating the feasibility of auto-immune hardware, a fledgling field known as **immunotronics**. I have provided a few notes and links on the course website and/or the course DVD.

2.2 | Living computers

I've already noted that the development of computer technologies has generally involved a quest for smaller size and greater speed. Natural systems have the advantage over electronics here, operating on size scales an order smaller than electronic circuits and at the high speeds associated with molecular reactions. You've seen that silicon-based biology has led to numerous computer applications and advances in AI. But future generations of computers may not be based on silicon at all, but on complex biological molecules. Why not build computers out of biological materials? Why not create a whole new field of **molecular electronics**? What about living computers?

Certain inconvenient facts stand in the way of this vision. Biological materials are generally too fragile and too difficult to work with to be the basis of systems that are reliable enough for everyday purposes. It is also very hard to interface them with electronic components. Nevertheless the first steps are now being taken towards living computers.

Protein memory

Much current research focuses on a particular protein, *bacteriohodospin* (bR). In living creatures, bR works as a molecular pump, transporting protons across cell membranes. When activated by light it produces energy in a cyclical photosynthetic process, with the molecule flipping between two energy states: the O state (in which it is dormant) and the Q state (in which it is producing energy). So it looks like a suitable medium for digital data storage – 1s and 0s.

A number of prototype data storage devices using bR have been produced. One of these uses bR molecules scattered densely through a thin film as an *associative memory* that works on the principle of the **hologram**. A laser beam is generated and then split into two beams. One of these, the *object beam*, encodes the data to be stored and is passed through a system that converts this into an array of pixels. The object beam is then reflected back to meet the other beam, the *reference beam*, within the bR film, which captures the characteristic holographic pattern formed by the interference between the two beams. The film can store millions of different memories in this way. Thus, when a beam encoding data is shone through the film in future, the bR film is able to *reconstruct* the beam that is closest to one of its stored patterns, in the manner of an associative memory.

You considered associative memories in Unit 2 of Block 4.

There have been a number of other experiments using bR as a digital memory. Again, I've provided some links on the course website and/or the course DVD.

DNA computation

Although still in their infancy, **DNA computers** can potentially store billions of times more data than a conventional computer, and solve the kind of difficult problems I've discussed throughout M366.

In 1994, Leonard Adleman, a computer scientist at the University of Southern California, introduced the idea of using DNA to solve complex mathematical problems. He devised an experiment in which DNA molecules were used to solve a seven-city Travelling Salesman Problem (TSP). Briefly, the steps in the experiment were as follows:

▶ The seven cities were represented by strands of DNA, using sequences of the molecular bases A, T, C and G to represent each city and possible routes.

▶ These molecules were then mixed in a test tube. The DNA strands tend to stick together. A chain of these strands can be taken to represent a possible answer.

▶ Within a few seconds, all of the possible combinations of DNA strands, each one representing a possible path, come together in the test tube.

▶ Other molecules were eliminated by various chemical processes, leaving only paths connecting all seven cities.

Although it was rather clumsy and slow, Adelman's experiment demonstrated the possibility of DNA computing. In 1997, a team at the University of Rochester developed logic gates made of DNA, the first step towards creating a molecular computer. Research continues steadily. By 2003, an Israeli team devised a programmable DNA computer capable of 330 trillion operations per second. In it, DNA molecules and enzymes combine in chemical reactions, each of which represents a simple computational step: the process is self-sustaining and self-regulating. However, the 'machine' was only capable of certain, fairly simple, functions. True DNA computing still lies a long way in the future.

Once again, you'll find notes and links to interesting sites related to molecular computation on the course website and/or the course DVD.

2.3 Artificial life

Some contemporary science writers speak of artificial life (or A-Life) as something completely new. They forget that the earliest computer scientists were intensely interested in the relationships between machines and living things. Alan Turing himself did major work in biology, seeking a precise mathematical account of morphogenesis. I've already mentioned John von Neumann's interest in self-replicating machines, and you looked at some of the properties of John Conway's Game of Life, a classic cellular automaton, in Block 3.

So what is artificial life (A-Life)? According to Christopher Langton, A-Life:

> ... complements the traditional biological sciences concerned with the *analysis* of living organisms by attempting to *synthesize* life-like behaviours within computers and other artificial media. By extending the empirical foundations upon which biology is based beyond the carbon-chain life that has evolved on Earth, artificial life can contribute to theoretical biology by locating *life-as-we-know-it* within the larger picture of *life-as-it-could-be*.

Source: Langton (1989)

Stated like this, the goal of A-Life is to abstract the 'logical form' of life, independent of the particulars of the carbon-based biological life forms that arose on this planet. The natural medium in which to do this would seem to be the computer.

Exercise 1.1

What do you think might be the benefits, theoretical and/or practical, of creating and studying A-Life?

Discussion ....

The benefits, both theoretical and practical, seem to fall into two categories. As a theoretical tool, A-Life may give biologists greater insights into some of the major problems of biology and biochemistry. At the same time it might benefit mathematicians, computer scientists, economists and others, by illuminating the workings of complex, dynamic, interactive systems.

In practical terms, we've already seen in Block 3 how insights from biology can be put to use in solving difficult computational problems of optimisation and control. In addition, A-Life may have practical results in many areas outside computing, including biochemistry, drug design and nanotechnology.

Many of the biologically inspired systems you've looked at in M366 might be seen as part of, or closely related to, the wider A-Life enterprise. Some biologists believe that it could be a powerful tool in the search for answers to some of the 'grand challenge' questions in biology and the environmental sciences, including:

▶ the origin of life;

▶ the evolution of complexity;

▶ the structure of ecosystems.

A vast range of different approaches to A-Life have been proposed. All share a common set of principles which were major themes of the biologically inspired AI approach described in Block 3:

▶ bottom-up rather than top-down modelling;

▶ local rather than global control;

▶ simple rather than complex specifications;

▶ emergent rather than pre-specified behaviour;

▶ simulation of populations rather than of individuals.

M366 has been a course on artificial *intelligence* rather than artificial *life*, so it's not appropriate to explore the field of A-Life any further. However, some thinkers believe that *life* and *intelligence* are strongly linked phenomena. This leads us to our second theme: how far might biologically inspired systems take us towards true intelligence?

ACTIVITY 1.1 (optional)

Within this activity on the course DVD you will find a number of links and resources to help you investigate further some of the above fields. If you have time, browse through some of these.

2.4 Afterword – cyborgs and transhumans

For completeness, a final word about these two notions. As with many currently trendy ideas, the concept of a **cyborg** (short for 'CYBernetic ORGanism') is scarcely a new one. In its dry, but useful way, the OED defines a cyborg as:

> a person whose physical tolerances or capabilities are extended beyond normal human limitations by a machine or other external agency that modifies the body's functions; an integrated man–machine system.

The term first appeared in an article of 1961 on the physiological implications of space flight, in which Manfred Clynes and Nathan Kline discussed the cybernetics of possible human–machine systems in space. The concept of some kind of fusion of human and machine has been a staple of science fiction for decades, and has been enthusiastically adopted in popular culture – in the Star Trek films, TV shows and on countless internet sites. I have just this minute typed 'cyborg' into Google and received 1.5 million hits.

The problem in any discussion of cyborgs is filtering the items of scientific interest from the vast ocean of nonsense that has been written on the subject. However, it is certainly fair to say that we can look forward to a future in which there will be a closer relationship between humans and electronic devices. We can see this happening already, in the shape of new research into wearable and ubiquitous computers. However, it is the field of medical applications for human subjects who have suffered various forms of disablement that offers the most likely prospects of possible cybernetic futures.

At its wildest, this line of thought has led some academics to suggest that the future that awaits us is **transhuman** – a new stage in human development. Predictably enough, the term 'transhuman' also originated in the 1960s, with a university teacher who had named himself FM-2030 (his real name was F.M. Esfandiary).

I've provided a small selection of web links to cyborg and transhuman sites, on the course website and/or the course DVD. You are welcome to make up your own minds about them.

3 Intelligent machines?

3.1 Recapitulating themes

It's time to wrap up M366. To do this, let's revisit one or two of the issues raised in Block 1 and try to tackle the cluster of questions I posed in the introduction to this unit: how far have we succeeded in creating intelligent machines? In what sense, if any, are the kinds of systems I've presented in the course 'intelligent'? Is it even *possible* to create an intelligent machine? If so, does the biologically inspired approach take us any further towards this goal than conventional symbolic strategies?

Before we start, we need to recall a few of the concepts and terms that I've introduced in M366.

SAQ 1.1

Write down what you understand by the following terms:

▶ intelligence

▶ Symbolic AI

▶ natural intelligence

▶ biologically inspired AI.

ANSWER..

In Block 1, you saw that there is no universally agreed definition of *intelligence*, but that the idea is often associated with the *human* capacity to think abstractly, reason, apply knowledge, use language, etc. I argued that it is easier to identify examples of intelligent behaviour than to define the concept itself, and that intelligent behaviour might be a means by which to recognise intelligence.

I defined *Symbolic AI* as 'a study of the technological questions surrounding the possible replication of human intelligence on digital computers, using principles of representation and search'. In Block 2, you learned that such representations were made explicit and came in the form of symbols. Search was the means by which AI systems attempted to simulate human reasoning using operations performed on symbols and symbol structures.

In Block 3, *natural intelligence* was defined in terms of the ability to solve problems without the need for symbolic reasoning. I suggested that a loose definition could be 'goal-directed, systematic, ordered problem-solving behaviour arising in complex systems, without the need for rationality, planning and explicit representation'. The generation of this kind of behaviour was explained in terms of the interplay of four mechanisms: interaction, emergence, adaptation and selection.

Finally, also in Block 3, I defined *biologically inspired AI* as 'the project to bring insights about the mechanisms underlying natural intelligence to difficult computational problems'.

One further point is worth bringing out here: Symbolic AI systems are based on the *physical symbol system hypothesis*, and thus make use of symbols as explicit representations, corresponding directly to entities in the world. In biologically inspired systems, representations are generally *implicit*. An example of an implicit representation would be a pattern of weights or activations in a neural network. Systems in which the tokens that are manipulated are not themselves symbols are generally referred to as **sub-symbolic systems**.

Let's also re-examine three topics that were briefly introduced in Block 1:

▶   simulation and replication

▶   strong and weak AI

▶   the Turing Test.

These three concepts will be crucial to my discussion.

Simulation and replication

In Block 1, you were introduced to the idea of a model as a simplified picture of reality. Models can be of various types, and I distinguished between models that are *simulations* and those that are *replications*. Models of biological intelligence, I claimed, were attempts at replication, in one form or another.

SAQ 1.2

Write down what you understand by the terms *simulation* and *replication*.

ANSWER...

A *simulation* of a system is a model that captures the functional connections between the inputs and outputs of the system.

A *replication* of a system is a model that captures these connections and is based on processes that are the same as, or similar to, those of the system being modelled.

To what extent, if at all, do AI systems replicate, as opposed to merely simulate, the kind of intelligence demonstrated by natural systems? In biologically inspired AI, the distinction between simulation and replication seems especially blurred. Unlike many Symbolic AI systems, biologically inspired systems do attempt to imitate the processes of the natural systems they model. But there is no agreement on how faithfully they do this: all models are simplifications, and biologically inspired systems are models in silicon of exceptionally complex organic systems. They seem to straddle the border between simulation and replication.

And does replication of an intelligent system mean that the replication will itself be intelligent? Naturally, nobody agrees on this either. According to some AI practitioners, true replication of an intelligent system is theoretically possible and such a system would indeed *be intelligent*. Others argue that creating intelligent behaviour by means of processes similar to those in corresponding natural systems only gives the *illusion* of intelligence to the outsider. The 'intelligence' – like beauty – is, they claim, wholly in the mind of the beholder. Genuine intelligence requires something more than the right kind of behaviour generated by appropriate processes. This point will come up time and time again in our discussions.

Strong and weak AI

The view that AI systems can replicate the intelligence of natural systems is related to the distinction between *strong* and *weak AI* I made in Block 1. Let's now return to this distinction.

SAQ 1.3

Write down what you understand by the terms 'strong AI' and 'weak AI'.

ANSWER...

In Block 1, I defined weak AI as a practical programme that aims to build computer systems with intelligent behaviour, but which are not necessarily based on human mental processes, nor claimed to be intelligent in any strong sense. Strong AI was defined as the imitation of human mental processes, with the aim of building computer systems that are truly intelligent in exactly the same way that humans are intelligent.

As you learned, the distinction was originally proposed by the philosopher John Searle in his classic 1980 paper, 'Minds, brains and programs'. Searle saw weak AI more as a tool for psychological investigations of intelligent processes in humans, than as the practical, engineering discipline for the construction of systems with intelligent behaviour it is now generally considered to be. But the distinction still stands. For Searle, strong AI made much more ambitious claims. Strong AI, according to him, is a theory of the mind in which the idea of a *program* is central. The actual hardware on which a system runs is irrelevant: provided the right program is running, then the system can be said not only to be intelligent, but to have a mind. Just as the human mind is assumed to be a program running on a particular piece of organic hardware – the brain – so, in strong AI, a suitably programmed computer can also be a mind. Strong AI asserts that, given the right programs, a computer can literally have cognitive states such as understanding, thinking, believing, and so on.

The idea that the mind is a program is a version of a theory known as **functionalism**. Functionalists believe that minds, including their intentionality, can entirely be explained in terms of computation. Thus, the theory is also sometimes termed **computationalism**, or the **computational model of the mind**. It is the view that computation is both necessary and sufficient for cognition (thinking, understanding, etc.).

You'll recall from Block 1 that computational theories of mind have a long history, originating in the seventeenth century with Thomas Hobbes.

Looking back over M366, it's clear that it has been overwhelmingly concerned with *weak* AI. I've viewed biologically inspired systems as a means by which to *understand* intelligence in natural systems (Block 3) and as a *technology* for solving problems – in optimisation, pattern recognition, programming and behavioural robotics (Blocks 3, 4 and 5) – based on the four mechanisms of interaction, adaptation, emergence and selection. However, I've claimed that the biologically inspired AI systems examined in the course were attempts at replications, rather than just simulations. Perhaps biologically inspired systems could – even *should* – also be interpreted as intelligent in a strong sense.

I'll return to Searle's conception of strong AI in the next section.

The Turing Test

As you learned in Block 1, two key issues for AI practitioners are determining what the defining features of intelligence are and how they can be recognised. You also know that Alan Turing introduced what he called the 'imitation game', which later became known as the 'Turing Test', to answer exactly these questions. So, given the possibility that biologically inspired systems might be considered intelligent in a strong as well as in a weak sense, we should look again at the Turing Test.

A useful online graphical resource summarising the Turing Test and examining its validity is available at http://www.macrovu.com/CCTWeb/.

SAQ 1.4

Briefly describe the Turing Test and what it is supposed to be testing.

ANSWER..

The Turing Test is a variant of a classic imitation game and involves three participants, a computer (A), a human being (B) and a human judge (C). All three are isolated from one other and A and B are only allowed to communicate with C through some printed means, such as a teletype. C has to try to determine which of A and B is the computer by asking them a series of questions and analysing the replies; if C cannot determine that A is the computer, then A is said to have 'passed' the test.

In Block 1, I traced a long tradition from Descartes to Turing that has taken the ability to communicate in natural language as the hallmark of intelligence. So the Turing Test's central claim is that it is possible to test for the presence of intelligence by testing for intelligent *behaviour* such as the capacity to hold conversations. But it must be obvious that the Turing Test is far from perfect. Consider this slightly challenging exercise.

Exercise 1.2

Suppose that a computer has 'passed' the Turing Test. There are at least three reasons why this might have happened. Spend a few minutes trying to identify what they are. (Hint: Think about the 'intelligence' of the three participants and the possibility that a participant might 'smarten up' or 'dumb down'.)

Discussion ....

Computer scientist Jaron Lanier, suggests that either:

► the computer may have 'smartened up' to the level of the human being; or

► the human being may have 'dumbed down' to the level of the computer; or

► the judge might have 'dumbed down' to the extent that he or she is incapable of differentiating between the computer and the human being.

So, the Turing Test, at least as originally conceived, can be passed in more than one way, only one of which requires the computer system to be genuinely intelligent. An even more important point is that the decision as to whether or not a system is genuinely intelligent, or merely *seems* 'intelligent', cannot be definitely settled. It is a test of behaviour judged to be intelligent in the subjective opinion of an observer. Such 'intelligence' could be pure illusion.

Let's now think about the Turing Test in the light of these criticisms and in the context of biologically inspired AI.

3.2 Revisiting the Turing Test

The Turing Test has never been without its critics. One AI practitioner, Blay Whitby, has described it as AI's 'biggest blind alley'. His observations are worth examining in a little detail.

You can read the full essay online at http://www.cogs.susx.ac.uk/users/blayw/tt.html.

Whitby begins by pointing to a common, yet mistaken, reading of Turing's paper, which assumes that the test was introduced to show that one could attempt to build an intelligent machine without a prior understanding of the nature of intelligence. He then goes on to argue that the idea that Turing's paper contains an adequate operational definition of intelligence is wrong:

> The paper was almost immediately read as providing an operational definition of intelligence [as] witnessed by the change from the label, 'imitation game' to 'Turing Test' by commentators. Turing himself was always careful to refer to 'the game'. The suggestion that it might be some sort of test involves an important extension of Turing's claims.
>
> Source: Whitby (1997)

Whitby then argues that this misinterpretation involves three mistaken assertions:

▶ Intelligence in computing machinery includes being able to deceive a human judge.

▶ The best approach to defining intelligence is through some sort of operational test, such as the 'imitation game'.

▶ Work specifically directed at producing a machine that can perform well in the 'imitation game' is genuine and useful AI research.

He goes on to suggest that assigning the label 'intelligent' to an entity is not a purely *technical* exercise, but is one that involves a range of *social* and *moral* dimensions. In Whitby's view, Turing's paper is really an exploration of *human attitudes*, rather than a definition of intelligence, and that the imitation game 'does not test for general intelligence, but for cultural similarity'. He concludes that the type of AI research that attempts to build systems capable of passing the Turing Test is best thought of as 'research into the mechanisms of producing certain sorts of illusion in human beings rather than anything to do with intelligence, artificial or otherwise'.

For Turing and others, thinking in a machine is presumed to be something that can be recognised *externally*, on the basis of observable behaviours such as language. And Turing was thinking of machines that *simulated* such behaviour by means of internal processes of representation and search. The Turing Test is flawed because it assumes that behaviour is a sufficient condition for identifying the presence of intelligence in a system. There is no reason why a purely simulated intelligence should not pass the test.

As you have seen throughout M366, biologically inspired AI is also motivated by the idea that there is an intimate connection between intelligence and behaviour. Unlike Symbolic AI, though, biologically inspired AI attempts to replicate, rather than merely simulate, intelligent behaviour, through interaction, emergence, adaptation and selection. But, since these four mechanisms can themselves be seen as forms of behaviour, biologically inspired AI is therefore concerned with behaviour at two levels:

▶ *macroscopic* or *high-level* behaviour, which is the behaviour of the system as a whole, emerging from:

▶ *microscopic* or *low-level* behaviour, the interactions of the component parts of the system, which generate the macroscopic behaviour.

So, a further question for us is this. Can the Turing Test be applied to biologically inspired systems that attempt to replicate intelligence, rather than simulate intelligent behaviour?

Exercise 1.3

Spend the next few minutes thinking about whether the Turing Test is applicable to biologically inspired AI.

Discussion ....

I thought that the Turing Test, at least as originally conceived, is not really applicable to biologically inspired AI, for at least two reasons:

▶ Firstly, it is anthropocentric (human-centred): it defines intelligence in terms of human capacities.

▶ Secondly, as you have seen, it merely tests for the presence of simulated intelligence, not replicated intelligence. Biologically inspired AI tries to replicate intelligence, not merely simulate it, using processes that lead to the emergence of intelligent behaviour in natural systems.

So, for the Turing Test to be applicable to biologically inspired AI, it would have to be modified in two ways:

▶ The anthropocentric bias of the test should be eliminated. The idea of intelligence that the test rests on must be decoupled from its association with human beings and generalised to biological systems. The kinds of behaviour the test looks for should no longer be specifically human abilities such as language, but instead tied up with behaviours characteristic of natural intelligence, such as the ability to respond and survive.

▶ As well as testing for naturally intelligent behaviour, the modified test should also determine whether the biologically inspired processes used to generate the behaviour are the same as those in the natural system.

Yet even if the Turing Test were modified along these lines, and a candidate system were to pass such a test, this would still not be nearly enough to convince some critics of strong AI. Let's now look at two of the key arguments.

3.3 | A critique of strong AI

Dreyfus's critique and the terms embodiment and situatedness were first introduced in Block 1.

In the next two sections, I will look at two classic arguments against strong AI: John Searle's Chinese Room Argument and Hubert Dreyfus's critique based on embodiment and situatedness. The arguments were originally formulated as attacks on strong *Symbolic AI*. But, as I've suggested, biologically inspired systems might well have a claim to be intelligent in the strong sense, too, so Searle's and Dreyfus's arguments may equally apply to them.

Searle and the Chinese Room

One further point to make about the Turing Test is that it is an *experiment*. Searle's Chinese Room Argument is also an experiment: a *thought* experiment.

Exercise 1.4

What do you think a 'thought experiment' might be? Do you think the Turing Test is a thought experiment, or some other type?

Discussion ....

A thought experiment is an *imagined situation* that is used to explore a set of ideas. Generally, such a situation could never actually be set up, either because it would be unethical, or because it would be impossible, practically or in principle. The Turing Test is not a thought experiment: it is a practical, or empirical, experiment, which can be, and is, carried out (remember the Loebner Prize in Block 1).

As you learned earlier, John Searle's definition of strong and weak AI first appeared in his seminal paper 'Minds, brains and programs' (1980). The Chinese Room Argument, introduced in the same paper, is intended to challenge two assumptions:

▶ that appropriate behaviour is a sufficient indicator of intelligence;

▶ the strong AI claim that a machine running the right kind of program can be said to have a mind.

Searle aims to do this by showing that it is perfectly possible for an AI system, running a program, to pass a test like the Turing Test in the absence of any real intelligence, and that it will lack at least one of the most basic features of a mind. In constructing the Chinese Room Argument, Searle deliberately focused on the *anthropocentric* and *linguistic* nature of the test, and set out to show how it was possible to *appear* to understand a language without genuinely understanding its meaning at all.

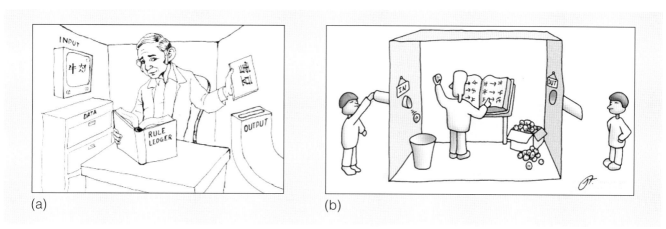

(a)   (b)

Figure 1.1   Two graphical depictions of the Chinese Room thought experiment; the one on the left features a caricature of John Searle, its inventor

Here is the Chinese Room thought experiment described by Searle in own words:

> Suppose that I'm locked in a room and given a large batch of Chinese writing. Suppose furthermore ... that I know no Chinese, either written or spoken, and that I'm not even confident that I could recognize Chinese writing as Chinese writing ... To me, Chinese writing is just so many meaningless squiggles.

> Now suppose further that after this first batch of Chinese writing I am given a second batch of Chinese script together with a set of rules for correlating the second batch with the first batch. The rules are in English, and I understand these rules as well as any other native speaker of English. They enable me to correlate one set of formal symbols with another set of formal symbols, and all that 'formal' means here is that I can identify the symbols entirely by their shapes. Now suppose also that I am given a third batch of Chinese symbols together with some instructions, again in English, that enable me to correlate elements of this third batch with the first two batches, and these rules instruct me how to give back certain Chinese symbols with certain sorts of shapes in response to certain sorts of shapes given me in the third batch. Unknown to me, the people who are giving me all of these symbols call the first batch 'a script,' they call the second batch a 'story' and they call the third batch 'questions.' Furthermore, they call the symbols

I give them back in response to the third batch 'answers to the questions,' and the set of rules in English that they gave me, they call 'the program.'

Now just to complicate the story a little, imagine that these people also give me stories in English, which I understand, and they then ask me questions in English about these stories, and I give them back answers in English. Suppose also that after a while I get so good at following the instructions for manipulating the Chinese symbols and the programmers get so good at writing the programs that from the external point of view ... my answers to the questions are absolutely indistinguishable from those of native Chinese speakers. Nobody just looking at my answers can tell that I don't speak a word of Chinese.

Let us also suppose that my answers to the English questions are, as they no doubt would be, indistinguishable from those of other native English speakers, for the simple reason that I am a native English speaker. From the external point of view – from the point of view of someone reading my 'answers' – the answers to the Chinese questions and the English questions are equally good. But in the Chinese case, unlike the English case, I produce the answers by manipulating uninterpreted formal symbols. As far as the Chinese is concerned, I simply behave like a computer; I perform computational operations on formally specified elements. For the purposes of the Chinese, I am simply an instantiation of the computer program.

Source: Searle (1980)

SAQ 1.5

Searle obviously intends the Chinese Room to be a metaphor for a computer system undergoing the Turing Test. In computer terms, what are the batches of squiggles passed into the room, the squiggles passed out of it and the book of rules for producing one set of squiggles in response to another?

ANSWER...

The incoming squiggles would be *inputs* in the form of stories and questions about these stories in a natural language. The outgoing squiggles are *outputs* in response to these inputs, also in a natural language. The book of rules is the *program* the computer uses to generate outputs from the inputs.

So what the Chinese Room Argument boils down to is this. A machine (the room) running a program (the book of rules for correlating one set of squiggles with another) can pass the Turing Test by producing perfectly convincing answers (the third batch of squiggles) to the Chinese questions (the second batch of squiggles) about the Chinese stories it is given (the first batch of squiggles), simply by applying the rules to the incoming squiggles and producing more squiggles in response. Yet to the machine, the squiggles have *no meaning whatsoever* – they are 'purely formal', 'uninterpreted'. The machine doesn't understand anything *about* the squiggles: it just blindly applies the rules.

A strange property of intentional mental states is that the things they are 'about' do not have to exist in the physical world: for example, I can think about unicorns, which do not, and never have, existed.

I need to introduce an important concept here. In any genuine mind, Searle argues, mental states must have **intentionality**. Intentionality is the property of certain mental states – thoughts, beliefs, desires, etc. – of being *about* objects or states of affairs in the world. For example, if I think about the summer sky my thought is *directed towards* the actual summer sky, and is *about* its blueness, depth, tranquillity, etc. The *content* of my thought about the summer sky is, in some way, the summer sky itself. Now, within the Chinese Room, Searle argues, the squiggles have no intentionality at all – they are not 'about' anything: they are just meaningless tokens. So, if meaning and intentionality are crucial to having a mind, then a machine just running a program cannot be said to have a mind.

Now think about the following exercise.

Exercise 1.5

If *syntax* refers to the relationships between the symbols of a language and *semantics* refers to the meaning of such symbols, what does the Chinese Room Argument imply about the relationship between syntax and semantics?

Discussion ....

The Chinese Room Argument is designed to show that syntax (the rules, or the program) is not sufficient for semantics (the meaning of the symbols). The meaning of the symbols of a language cannot be a product of the syntactic relationships between them.

Searle never intended the Chinese Room Argument to show that there cannot be artificial thinking machines. On the contrary, he states there is at least one kind of machine that can think – human beings. Rather, he intended the argument to show that no digital computer can understand, or have any other genuine psychological characteristics, solely in virtue of running a program. The argument is not just aimed at the Turing Test, but also at Turing's original conception of a computing machine. I discussed Turing's original analysis of the computer, and Haugeland's version of it, as an interpreted automatic formal system, in Block 1. The *formal* aspect of computation now comes back to haunt us: formal symbols have no intrinsic meaning, and meaning is essential for mind, understanding and intelligence.

Nearly three decades on, the Chinese Room Argument still provokes an immense volume of debate, and remains an important weapon in the armoury of opponents of strong AI – at least of strong Symbolic AI. Searle anticipated a few of the many onslaughts his argument has suffered in his original paper, and included his responses to them there. In the next section, I'll look again at the Chinese Room Argument, examining some of the criticisms that have been raised against it, and consider how it might apply to biologically inspired AI.

A collection of articles debating the validity of the thought experiment can be found in Preston and Bishop (2002).

First, though, we should turn our attention to the second of the two classic arguments against strong AI: Dreyfus's critique based on embodiment and situatedness.

Dreyfus – a critique of cognitive reason

The philosopher Hubert Dreyfus also appeared briefly in Block 1. His 1979 book, *What Computers Can't Do*, updated and republished in 1993 as *What Computers* Still *Can't Do*, is a powerful attack on strong AI.

The subtitle of this book is *A critique of cognitive reason* and I'm borrowing it for the title of this section.

In Symbolic AI, thinking (including having mental states such as beliefs, goals, plans, etc.) involves manipulating (usually by search) explicit representations, composed of discrete symbols and symbol structures – frames, scripts, semantic networks, etc. But Dreyfus contests the idea that all knowledge can be expressed in the form of explicit symbolic representations. Any attempt to capture common-sense knowledge and reasoning in collections of *rules* is, he contends, doomed to fail. Rules cannot capture the richness of experience.

Dreyfus argues that understanding is not something that is tied up with mental representations and their manipulation in the head. It is a *bodily skill* and such skills are based on *patterns*, not rules. For Dreyfus, many human concerns cannot be captured in the form of explicit goals, since these often become explicit only *after* they have been fulfilled. Human concerns pervade our experience, and when they are made explicit, they lose their pervasive character.

Dreyfus presents an alternative to Symbolic AI's conception of intelligence, based on the idea that intelligent creatures have *bodies* that are *situated* in a complex world. The purpose of their intelligence is to help them handle this world successfully. You'll recall that this is very much the line I took when we considered natural intelligence in Block 3. On this situated and embodied view, intelligent human action in the world involves *coping* with *equipment* – using tools in pursuing practical projects – rather than relating to the world through mental representations. Such coping skills cannot be reduced to formal rules. Coping takes place against a background of general familiarity with the way things are, on the basis of which we are able to decide what is relevant, what to pay attention to, and what to do in any given situation. Human intelligence consists of responding to situations similar to situations encountered in the past, in ways similar to ones that have worked well in the past. But neither 'situations' nor 'similarity' can be specified in terms of rules or symbols.

We can summarise the main points of Dreyfus's argument against Symbolic AI by stating that Symbolic AI has the following flaws:

▶ It attempts to represent discrete, abstract concepts; however, knowledge is 'fuzzy', context sensitive or *situational*, and holistic.

▶ It deals in micro-theories about abstract microworlds (think of Blocks World); however, our knowledge of the world is concrete and *embodied*.

▶ It pins its hopes on huge databases of propositional knowledge; however, the bulk of our knowledge concerns *usage* not *facts*.

You can see that Dreyfus's notions of *embodiment* and *situatedness* are basic features of my proposals about natural intelligence in Block 3, and to much of the biologically inspired approach to AI. We will examine both of these ideas more closely later in the block. But first I need to bring out one issue that lies at the heart of both Searle's and Dreyfus's arguments – the problem of *grounding* and *meaning*.

Grounding and meaning

The Chinese Room Argument was designed to show that the meaning of the symbols of a language cannot arise from the syntactic relationships between them. Dreyfus urged the importance of embodiment and situatedness to human understanding. Meaning, embodiment and situatedness are all tied up in the issue of **grounding**.

Grounding refers to the way in which meaning is established in a system. Two types of grounding appear in the AI literature – *symbol grounding* and *physical grounding*.

If an artificial agent makes use of symbolic representations, and if that agent is to be called intelligent, then such representations must be *grounded*: they have to be given meaning in some way. Remember again Haugeland's definition of a digital computer as an interpreted automatic formal system. In Haugeland's analysis, computer symbols are indeed given meaning – they are interpreted – but only from *outside the system*. Meaning can only come from the human users and operators of the computer. How can the symbols of a computer system have meaning for *the system itself*? This is the **symbol grounding problem**, neatly expressed by cognitive scientist Stevan Harnad as follows:

> How can the semantic interpretation of a formal symbol system be made intrinsic to the system, rather than just parasitic on the meanings in our heads? How can the meanings of the meaningless symbol tokens, manipulated solely on the basis of their (arbitrary) shapes, be grounded in anything but other meaningless symbols?

Source: Harnad (1995)

As Searle showed, mere symbol manipulation is not enough for meaning. Cognitive scientists generally take the view that symbols are grounded by the relations they have with one another, and with the things in the world they refer to. For example, the symbol 'dog' carries the meaning *dog* because of the relation between the symbol and the presence of real dogs in the external world. The meaning of 'Rover', a symbol representing a particular dog, gets some of its meaning from its relation to the ground symbol 'dog'. This style of explanation is termed **symbol grounding**.

Other AI practitioners, such as roboticist Rodney Brooks, have argued that while symbol grounding is indeed a problem, it is **physical grounding** that is critical to intelligence. Physical grounding is the idea that a system is grounded if it is situated within, and intimately connected to, the physical world. Unlike symbol grounding, which involves symbols mediating the connection between an agent and its environment, physical grounding involves the direct coupling of a non-symbolic embodied agent to its environment.

SAQ 1.6

Write brief definitions of symbol grounding and physical grounding. What do you think is the main difference between the two types of grounding?

ANSWER...

Both symbol grounding and physical grounding involve the coupling of an agent to its environment. In the case of physical grounding, the coupling is direct, while in the case of symbol grounding, it is through symbols.

Note that the symbol grounding problem and proposals for solving it have been formulated with the assumption that the semantic interpretation of a system *can* be made intrinsic to the system. This can be disputed.

Equipped with an understanding of the idea of grounding, and of the symbol grounding problem, we can go on to explore some of the possible replies to Searle's and Dreyfus's arguments.

3.4　Strong AI and the Chinese Room

Searle's and Dreyfus's work have attracted many responses from AI researchers, philosophers and cognitive psychologists. Searle himself anticipated some of these and included answers to them in his 1980 and later papers. I'll consider two of the most important in this section, and one in the next.

The system reply

One of the immediate responses to the Chinese Room Argument was to argue that although the person in the room does not understand Chinese, the entire *system* – the person, rule book, bits of paper, the room itself – of which the person is merely one *component* does, in fact, understand it. Searle had anticipated this reply and presented a counter-response in 'Minds, brains and programs':

> Let the individual internalize all of these elements of the system. He memorizes the rules in the ledger and the data banks of Chinese symbols, and he does all the calculations in his head. The individual then incorporates the entire system. There isn't anything at all to the system that he does not encompass. We can

even get rid of the room and suppose he works outdoors. All the same, he understands nothing of the Chinese, and *a fortiori* neither does the system, because there isn't anything in the system that isn't in him.

Source: Searle (1980)

Searle's reply has itself been criticised on the grounds that it is not logically sound. Consider the following re-statement of his argument:

1   The system is part of the individual.

2   If the individual does not understand Chinese then no part of the individual understands Chinese.

3   The formal symbol manipulation carried out by the individual does not enable the individual to understand Chinese.

4   Therefore, the formal symbol manipulation carried out by the individual does not enable the system to understand Chinese.

According to some commentators, step 2 is highly questionable. They argue that it is quite possible that some module in the person's head – a component of the system that was previously external to the person and which has now been internalised by them – might be able to understand Chinese without the person being able to do so. However, while it is true that parts of a system can have properties that the system as a whole does not possess, it does not follow that such parts include the ability to understand.

The Robot Reply

In the Robot Reply, imagine the room is equipped with sensory and motor channels between the symbol manipulator inside and the external world. Then symbol manipulation *and* appropriate coupling to the world through the two channels might give meaning to the symbols processed within the room. The Robot Reply embodies the idea of symbol grounding: for the system as a whole to understand, there needs to be the right kind of relations between the symbols in the program and the things they refer to in the external world.

Again, Searle anticipated this reply in the 'Minds, brains and programs' article and presented the following as a counter-response:

The answer to the Robot Reply is that the addition of such 'perceptual' and 'motor' capacities adds nothing by way of understanding, in particular, or intentionality, in general, to [the] original program. To see this, notice that the same thought experiment applies to the robot case. Suppose that instead of the computer inside the robot, you put me inside the room and, as in the original Chinese case, you give me more Chinese symbols with more instructions in English for matching Chinese symbols to Chinese symbols and feeding back Chinese symbols to the outside. Suppose, unknown to me, some of the Chinese symbols that come to me come from a television camera attached to the robot and other Chinese symbols that I am giving out serve to make the motors inside the robot move the robot's legs or arms.

It is important to emphasize that all I am doing is manipulating formal symbols: I know none of these other facts. I am receiving 'information' from the robot's 'perceptual' apparatus, and I am giving out 'instructions' to its motor apparatus without knowing either of these facts. I am the robot's homunculus, but unlike the traditional homunculus, I don't know what's going on. I don't understand anything except the rules for symbol manipulation. Now in this case I want to say that the robot has no intentional states at all; it is simply moving about as a result of its electrical wiring and its program. And furthermore, by instantiating the program I have no intentional states of the relevant type. All I do is follow formal instructions about manipulating formal symbols.

Source: Searle (1980)

Here, Searle seems to be proposing that the symbol manipulator is completely decoupled from the robot . He also appears to ignore the active, *exploratory* nature of an autonomous robot. As a number of critics have argued, the intentionality of the robot comes from the coupling of the whole system with the world. It is the symbol manipulator *and* the symbols *and* the sensors and actuators *considered as a whole* that is an intentional system, capable of understanding. A robotic AI system of this type would, according to its proponents, be able to solve the symbol grounding problem and could thus possess true intelligence.

This was highlighted in Case Study 3.5 in Unit 3 of Block 5, and elsewhere.

On this basis, Stevan Harnad proposes an extension to the Turing Test – the 'Total Turing Test'. A candidate system is required to be able to do all the things that human beings can do, to be able to *perceive* (through the use of sensors) and *act* (through the use of actuators) in and on the world. According to Harnad, although the Chinese Room Argument discredits strong Symbolic AI, it does not discredit strong *robotic* AI: if a robotic system 'sees' an object, then it *really* does see it, as it has appropriate visual sensors. However, this view has been contested by cognitive scientists Selmer Bringsjord and Ron Noel on the grounds that, once again, there is a distinction between seeing *without* understanding and seeing *with* understanding; according to them, robotic systems are capable of the former, but not the latter.

Exercise 1.6

Spend the next few minutes thinking about the dispute between Searle, his supporters and his critics. Try to identify the source of this dispute. (Hint: You might want to look again at Searle's and Harnad's respective positions on the symbol grounding problem.)

Discussion ....

I thought that the dispute arises from radically different ideas about the nature of meaning. For Searle's critics, meaning lies in the coupling between an agent and its world. For Searle and his supporters, it lies in the agent's head – or more precisely, in its *mind*. Technically, Harnad's position is based on **externalist semantics**, and on Searle's **internalist semantics**. Searle maintains that it is not symbol *grounding* that is important but symbol *meaning*, and this is not generated through the coupling of symbols to a sensor–actuator interface – it comes from intentionality, which is necessarily tied to consciousness.

You might now be wondering whether there is any way through this apparent impasse. One possibility is to consider other types of robotic AI, such as the biologically inspired sub-symbolic robotic systems you learned about in Blocks 3 and 5.

3.5 Biologically inspired AI and the Chinese Room

Biologically inspired systems, and especially robotic systems, look as if they might be able to bypass the symbol grounding problem. Their sub-symbolic nature makes it very difficult to analyse them in terms of syntax and semantics, and thus makes it harder to construct Chinese Room Arguments against them. And since it is in *neural networks* that symbols seem to play the least, if any, role, robotic agents controlled by neural networks (see Block 5) would seem most likely to be immune to such arguments.

Neural networks and the Chinese Gym

You examined the principles and techniques of artificial neural networks (ANNs) in detail in Block 4. In this section I will discuss the possibility that neural systems are capable of defeating the Chinese Room Argument, and thus getting us closer to our goal of building intelligent machines. Let's begin by reviewing one of the conceptual foundations of neural networks.

Both neural and Symbolic AI systems run on digital computers, so they are both examples of computational systems, in which the fundamental syntactic entities are *computational tokens* – objects that are manipulated in order for computation to take place – and the fundamental semantic entities are *representations*.

SAQ 1.7

What are the computational tokens and representations in an ANN?

ANSWER..

In an ANN, the computational tokens are individual activations and connections. The principal representations, however, are emergent, distributed patterns of activation over whole sets of units. Thus neural representations are not discrete and atomic, unlike the representations in Symbolic AI systems. In these, the computational tokens are symbols and the representations are the interpretations placed on the symbols.

Neural networks belong to the class of *sub-symbolic AI* systems I identified earlier. In a symbolic system, the computational level is the same as the representational level: the objects of syntactic manipulation are also objects of semantic interpretation. In a sub-symbolic system, the computational level lies beneath the semantic, representational level. For example, the individual activations or weights in an ANN are not representations in their own right: they only carry meaning as part of some overall *pattern* of activations or weights.

The Brain Simulator Reply to the Chinese Room Argument is based on these insights. A computational system that simulated the complete pattern of neuronal connections and firings of a Chinese speaker would, it is argued, be able to understand Chinese.

However, this reply was also anticipated by Searle. He asks us to imagine that the room contains a huge system of water pipes, simulating the pattern of neurons in the brain of a Chinese speaker. Now imagine that the person in the Chinese Room is given a new rule book that tells them how to operate the system. When the person receives Chinese input, they look up in the English rule book which valves to turn on and off, and the system eventually squirts out a Chinese response. Even though the water pipes simulate the formal (that is, structural) properties of the Chinese speaker's brain, the person controlling them has no understanding of Chinese.

Searle later introduced the **Chinese Gym Argument**, a variant of the Chinese Room adapted to apply to systems such as ANNs:

> Imagine that instead of a Chinese Room, I have a Chinese Gym: a hall containing many monolingual English-speaking men. These men would carry out the same operations as the nodes and synapses [i.e. units and connections] in a connectionist architecture ... [The] outcome would be the same as having

one man manipulate symbols according to a rule book. No one in the gym speaks a word of Chinese, and there is no way for the system as a whole to learn the meaning of any Chinese words. Yet with appropriate adjustments, the system would give correct answers to Chinese questions.

Source: Searle (1990)

The Chinese Gym idea seems to invite the instant reply that it takes no account of *emergence*: after all, no individual neuron in my head understands English, yet somehow the system as a whole does. David Chalmers argues that the problem of the Chinese Room (or Chinese Gym) can be addressed by appealing to the structure of the patterns of activation that emerge in neural networks. Interesting patterns emerge at the macroscopic level from interactions between units at the microscopic level.

It is hoped that as a consequence of following rules [at the sub-symbolic] level, semantic properties will emerge – that is, manifest themselves in the processing and behaviour of the program – without having been explicitly programmed in.

Source: Chalmers (1992)

In other words, emergent distributed representations can carry meaning by virtue of the rich internal *structure* of complex patterns of activation. Chalmers calls this *internal grounding* and maintains that, unlike symbol grounding, this type of grounding involves the same type of internalist semantics to which Searle is committed – meaning that is 'in the head'.

However, Searle would reply that identifying an internal structure and correlating it with meaning is a process that depends, as always, on an external observer. And for him, meaning is at least partly a *subjective*, **first-person phenomenon**, whereas a structure is *objective* or a **third-person phenomenon**. Thus an appeal to the internal structure of patterns of activation in ANNs is an inadequate reply. Chalmers is right to place semantics 'in the head', Searle would say; but he still locates it wrongly. He places it in the brain, whereas it is in the *mind* – in *consciousness*.

Third-person phenomena are ones that can, in principle, be observed by anyone: 'it's raining', 'there is a giraffe over there', etc. First-person phenomena can only be observed by me: 'I'm hungry', 'my big toe itches', etc.

Perhaps the fairest and most balanced conclusion to all this is that a combination of the Robotic Reply and the Neural Network replies to the Chinese Room Argument looks the strongest. Non-symbolic, biologically inspired, neurally controlled robotic systems of the kind discussed in Blocks 3 and 5 seem to be most resistant to Chinese Room type criticism. They may offer the best route to our goal of creating intelligent machines.

3.6 Biologically inspired AI – embodiment, situatedness and embeddedness

The most serious criticism of the Turing Test in its original form is that it is 'intellectualist': it ignores what is *really* important about intelligent behaviour – the ability to adapt and survive in the real world through coordinated perception and action. Dreyfus's attack on strong AI, his argument from embodiment and situatedness, is based entirely on this premise. How do biologically inspired systems fare here?

Reactive robotic AI systems appear to possess both of these abilities on account of their being sub-symbolic, embodied systems that are physically grounded, coupled directly to the world via sensors and actuators. In the previous section, you saw how this type of grounding might avoid Chinese Room style arguments. So it's likely that embodiment of this kind – physical being in, and direct coupling to, the world – is necessary for strong AI. But even if we assume that embodiment is *necessary* for intelligence, is it *sufficient*? In order to tackle this question, we will need to consider some criticisms of behaviour-based robotic AI. However, first briefly review your understanding of this topic.

Shakey appeared in Unit 3 of Block 2, while Ambler and Toto were both discussed in Unit 3 of Block 3.

SAQ 1.8

List the main differences between symbolic robotic AI systems (e.g. Shakey, Ambler) and behaviour-based robotic AI systems (e.g. Toto, neurally controlled systems in Block 5).

ANSWER...

Table 1.1 contains a list of the main differences between symbolic robotic AI systems of the kind described in Block 2 and behaviour-based robotic AI systems of the type described in Blocks 3 and 5.

Table 1.1   Comparison of symbolic robotic AI systems and behaviour-based robotic AI systems

Symbolic robotic AI	Reactive robotic AI
Sophisticated reasoning in impoverished domains. The hope is that the ideas used will generalise to robust behaviour in more complex domains.	Less sophisticated tasks performed robustly in complex domains. The hope is that the ideas used will generalise to more sophisticated tasks.
Relies on the use of heuristics to control search in functional modules.	Relies on the emergence of global, distal behaviour from the interaction of smaller units.
Goals and plans are designed in.	Behaviour is designed in, or learned, or evolved.
Behavioural responses are emergent.	(Apparent) goals and plans are emergent.
Constructs models of the world.	Uses the world as its own best model.
Involves symbol grounding.	Involves physical grounding.
Makes use of explicit (symbolic) representations that are centralised, manipulable and used to mediate the relation of the agent with the world.	Makes use of implicit (non-symbolic) representations that are decentralised, non-manipulable and defined through interactions of agents with the world.
Operates based on a SENSE–PLAN–ACT cycle.	Operates based on a SENSE–ACT cycle.
Constructed all at once in a top-down fashion.	Constructed incrementally or evolved in a bottom-up fashion.

Let us now consider some criticisms that can be, and have been, directed at biologically inspired behaviour-based robotic AI.

The emergence of goals

In Block 3, you looked at robotic AI systems in which seemingly goal-directed behaviour emerges from the interactions of simpler non-goal-directed behaviours. All the goals of such systems are eventually expressed as physical action.

One objection to this view is that such 'simpler non-goal-directed behaviours' may, in fact, be goal-directed themselves. Consider Brooks's use of goal-directed language to describe the low-level behaviour of system modules – AVOID, WANDER, FOLLOW-WALL, etc. Higher-level (*systemic*) goals appear to be emergent from lower-level (*component*) goals, so we might argue that goal-directedness does not emerge from something that is not goal-directed, but rather that *explicit* goal-directedness emerges from *implicit* goal-directedness. However, it's difficult to see how such an argument applies to neurally controlled robots.

Brooks's understanding and use of the idea of goal-directedness seems to be a variation on what philosopher Daniel Dennett has called the *intentional stance*. To take up the intentional stance is to view the behaviour of something in terms of its supposed mental properties. Dennett summarises the essence of the intentional stance as follows:

> Here is how it works: first you decide to treat the object whose behavior is to be predicted as a rational agent; then you figure out what beliefs that agent ought to have, given its place in the world and its purpose. Then you figure out what desires it ought to have, on the same considerations, and finally you predict that this rational agent will act to further its goals in the light of its beliefs. A little practical reasoning from the chosen set of beliefs and desires will in most instances yield a decision about what the agent ought to do; that is what you predict the agent will do.

Source: Dennett (1987)

So, for example, if I watch a cockroach walking around an obstacle towards some food, or a bird flying off as a shadow approaches, it's useful to think of their behaviour in terms of mental states. The cockroach *wants* to reach the food because it is *hungry*, and it *knows* it cannot climb over the obstacle. The bird *fears* the shadow, because it *believes* it is a cat. We all think like this, and sometimes even treat inanimate objects this way.

However, Dennett only considered the intentional stance to be useful for purposes of *prediction*: just because assuming something has mental states is useful in deciding what it is going to do next, it does not mean that the thing actually has such states. Brooks seems to go further than this, and makes use of the idea of goals as *explanations*. Although he often maintains that the apparent goals that emerge from his robotic systems are only *post facto* rationalisations of the behaviour arising from interactions between behaviours and the world, he also affirms that goals are *implicit* in such couplings.

In conclusion, we might say that the emergence of goal-directedness in Brooks's behaviour-based robots is best understood as the system making explicit what was implicit in its design all along. The sensor–motor couplings in robotic systems are *designed* by their human creators, and so reflect the *embedding* of human choices and understanding in them. Paraphrasing Stevan Harnad, we might say that the meaning of the behaviour generated by behaviour-based robotic AI systems appears to be 'parasitic on the meanings in our heads'. Once again, though, it is less clear how this line of argument applies to robotic systems that are neurally controlled, and adaptive or evolved.

However, there is one further line of criticism. It focuses on the importance of concepts in higher level intelligences, and especially human intelligence; and it is to this issue that I'll now turn.

Situatedness and embeddedness

In the previous section, I examined Dreyfus's appeal for embodiment in relation to biologically inspired robotic AI. In this section, I will explore his notion of **situatedness** in detail, and introduce a new idea – **embeddedness**.

Let's start with an exercise.

Exercise 1.7

Think about the terms 'situation' and 'context'. Try to identify some of the different types of situations and contexts that occur in everyday life.

Discussion ....

I defined a situation as a 'state of affairs' or 'set of circumstances'. The terms 'context' and 'situation' seem pretty much interchangeable. I thought of at least three different types of situation or context:

▶ *physical* or *task-based* (including artefacts and external representations of information);

▶ *environmental* or *ecological* (such as workplace or marketplace);

▶ *social* or *interactional* (as in educational instruction or clinical settings).

The situated perspective on intelligent human behaviour sees it as taking place not only within a physical environment, but also in countless *social* settings. It is not an abstract, detached, general-purpose process of logical or formal reasoning. One central insight is that the physical setting can greatly reduce the load of a cognitive agent by providing external cues about what to do next and when goals are accomplished.

Cognitive scientist and philosopher Brian Cantwell Smith summarises the main differences between the classical symbolic and situated approaches to cognition as follows:

Cognition in the classical approach is:

▶ *individual*: intelligence is taken to be a property of a solitary agent;

▶ *rational*: logical, conceptual thought is viewed as the essence of cognition;

▶ *abstract*: the physical environment is treated as of secondary importance (if relevant at all);

▶ *detached*: thinking is treated separately from perception and action;

▶ *general*: cognitive science is taken to be the search for universal principles of general reasoning, true of all individuals in all circumstances.

Cognition in the situated approach is:

▶ *social*: takes place in humanly constructed settings among human communities;

▶ *embodied*: the material aspects of agent's bodies are taken to be significant;

▶ *concrete*: physical constraints are viewed as of the utmost importance;

▶ *located*: all human endeavour depends on the context in which it takes place;

▶ *engaged*: there is continual interaction with the surrounding environment;

▶ *specific*: what people do varies dramatically, depending on their particular circumstances.

AI researchers recognise the force of this analysis. According to Brooks, 'if we are to build a robot with human-like intelligence then it must have a human-like body in order to be able to develop similar sorts of representations'. Furthermore, most agree that such a robot would need to be placed in situations similar to those that humans encounter in order to have similar 'experiences' and develop (evolve, learn, adapt, etc.) similarly.

Thus, for Brooks and others, intelligence requires embodiment and situatednesss. However, not everyone is so sure. According to cognitive scientist Ron Chrisley, proponents of embodied AI:

> ... rightly extol the virtues of situatedness, but are less forthcoming in their analysis of its vices. The fact is, there's a trade-off between speed and generality. The more one optimises one's methods to exploit contingencies of the environment, the more one's success is bound to those contingencies; change the context only a little and the situated routine fails, usually in a spectacularly stupid way.
>
> Source: Chrisley (2003)

However, there is a more pressing problem. Designers of reactive robots tend to see situatedness exclusively in *physical* terms; but I identified at least three different types of situation: physical, environmental and social. Therefore, some commentators, such as sociologist Harry Collins, distinguish between situatedness in the physical sense and *embeddedness*, or socialisation, which is a social–cultural phenomenon having to do with shared ways of life among the members of communities of embodied individuals. It is the capacity of humans to attain social fluency in one or more cultures. It is worth examining the development of Collins's position in a little detail.

Collins begins by summarising Dreyfus's critique of Symbolic AI:

> So long as computers don't have bodies they won't be able to do what we do; so long as computers represent the world in discrete lumps they won't be able to respond to the world in our way; we are always *in* a situation, whereas a computer only 'knows' its situation from a set of necessary and sufficient features.
>
> Source: Collins (1996)

But he then goes on to argue that, contrary to Dreyfus:,

> Given the capacity for linguistic socialisation, an individual can come to share a form of life without having a body or the experience of physical situations which correspond to that form of life.
>
> Source: Collins (1996)

So for Collins, language is all one needs for socialisation; bodies are irrelevant. He proposed a simple test – the ability of an AI to *repair* typed English conversations. As with the conventional Turing Test, this requires a determined judge who is not easily fooled, an intelligent and literate human control who shares the broad cultural background of the judge, and a machine with which the control is to be compared. The judge provides both the control and the machine with copies of a few typed paragraphs of misspelled and otherwise corrupted English. It is important that the paragraphs have not previously been seen, either by the control, or by the machine, or by the designers of the machine.

Once presented, the control and the machine are given an hour to render the passages into normal English. The judge will then be given the printed texts and will have to work out which has been amended by the control and which by the machine.

Here is a specimen of the sort of paragraph a judge would present to both the control and the machine:

Mary: Can you spell a word that means a religious ceremony?

John: You mean rite. Do you want me to spell it out loud?

Mary: No, I want you to write it.

John: I'm tired. All you ever want me to do is write, write, write.

Mary: That's unfair, I just want you to write, write, write.

John: OK, I'll write, write.

Mary: Write.

Now try the following exercise.

Exercise 1.8

Transliterate the above paragraph into normal English, repairing all the mistakes.

Answer..

Mary: Can you spell a word that means a religious ceremony?

John: You mean rite. Do you want me to spell it out loud?

Mary: No, I want you to write it.

John: I'm tired. All you ever want me to do is write, write, write.

Mary: That's unfair, I just want you to write 'rite', right?

John: OK, I'll write 'rite'.

Mary: Right.

The test is designed to draw on all the culture-bound common sense needed for error correction in printed English; and so the 'correct' response may vary from place to place and time to time. Collins maintained that such a test is quite sufficient to enable us to tell the socialised from the unsocialised. He argued that if a machine could pass a carefully designed version of this test, all the *significant* problems of AI would have been solved.

Collins's position was based on the following line of reasoning: if it is possible for people with non-standard bodies, such as the disabled, to acquire common-sense social knowledge, then it should be possible for a computer, with its own non-standard body, to acquire the same knowledge. However, Dreyfus has criticised this view, arguing that disabled individuals bear no resemblance to computers, and possess enough of a body structure to enable them to be socialised into our human world. Collins's later works admit the importance of some degree of embodiment to embeddedness.

The challenge of exposing robots to human culture through ordinary processes of socialisation, and seeing whether social abilities are acquired, has been taken up by many groups of roboticists. Rodney Brooks and his team at the MIT Artificial Intelligence Laboratory developed a robot, Cog, equipped with a torso, arms, legs and a head with 'eyes' and 'ears' that can move in various directions, and which was designed to go through an embodied infancy and childhood. The objective of the Cog project is nothing short of strong biologically inspired AI at the human level. However, Brooks has himself anticipated problems. For example:

> It is difficult to establish hard and fast criteria for what it might mean to *act like a human* – roughly we mean that the robot should act in such a way that an average (whatever that might mean) human observer would say that it is acting in a human-like manner, rather than a machine-like or alien-like manner.

Source: Brooks (1997)

Further details on the Cog project can be found at http://www.ai.mit.edu/projects/humanoid-robotics-group/cog/.

You may also remember case studies from Block 3 on social robotics (Case Studies 3.3 and 3.4) and human–robot interaction (Case Study 4.6). Groups from around the world are now working on projects in these fields. I have suggested some links on the course website and/or the course DVD.

3.7 Biologically inspired AI and Symbolic AI – the route map

The problem

M366 has presented two visions of AI. On the one hand, there is Symbolic AI, generally dealing with the simulation of very high-level human intelligent behaviour: planning, language, expert analysis, solving differential equations, etc. On the other, there is biologically inspired AI, based on the more inclusive idea of natural intelligence, and building systems with quite different capacities: pattern recognition, simple goal-directed behaviour, self-organisation, and so on. Both are important. No one disputes that the ultimate goal of AI is to build systems that can do really clever things, and perhaps eventually interact with humans as equals. And many practitioners of Symbolic AI would also admit that their field is ultimately too arid and abstract – concentrating too much on the classical assumptions about cognition outlined by Smith above, and paying too little attention to the situated and embedded aspects of intelligence acting in the world.

So here is the problem. In Block 3 I stated the view that life, and intelligence too, probably lies along some kind of *continuum*, from the simplest organisms and the most basic reactive behaviour, all the way through to the human intellect. Symbolic AI works at one end of that continuum, biologically inspired AI at the other. Where there is little work, and little understanding, is in the vast space between. How do we bridge the gulf between symbolic and sub-symbolic types of intelligence? How can we find a *route map* that charts the path from the low-level capacities associated with sub-symbolic natural intelligence – pattern recognition, non-symbolic communication and motor action – to the high-level, symbolic capacities of the human mind? This is a problem that a future science and technology will have to solve – assuming it is possible at all.

Rodney Brooks and others have argued that it will never be possible to understand human intelligence until we properly understand the workings of the simpler intelligences from which it evolved. There is a lot of truth in this, although the work has scarcely begun. But note that his belief conceals one crucial assumption – that human intelligence is of the same *kind* as the 'intelligence' of lower organisms, and that the behaviour-based approach is thus scaleable to human-level intelligence. There is much controversy over this, some of which centres on the question of the role *concepts* play in intelligence.

The role of concepts in intelligence

A number of critics have contested Brooks's assumption that intelligence is distributed along a continuum. Some argue that human intellect has a special place and unique qualities, going far beyond mere embodiment. For example, philosopher Mortimer Adler states that:

> In the life of all other animals, mind is embodied completely. Mind is found entirely embedded in physical organs. Mind is *in* matter. Only in man does mind rise *above* matter or *over* matter, by virtue of man's having a mind that has intellectual as well as sensitive powers, conceptual as well as perceptual thought, the power to think about what is unperceived and totally imperceptible,
>
> Source: Adler (1990)

In Unit 1 of Block 3, I drew attention to the central place that concepts have in human cognition, and suggested that higher animals might have rudimentary conceptual systems too. Cognitive scientist David Kirsch has taken up this theme. In his article 'Today the earwig, tomorrow man?', he questions many of the assumptions of pure biologically inspired AI. Kirsch maintains that 'although AI can substantially benefit from greater attention to the richness of perceptual information, this richness will never replace the need for internal representations.' He claims that two abilities are vital components of human intelligence – the ability to:

▶ *abstract*: that is, to organise experience into categories (concepts), so my friends Rover, Towser, Fido and Pooch all get assigned to the general class *dog*;

▶ *predicate*: that is, to associate properties with these concepts, and with their members, so dogs (and thus Rover, Towser, etc.) are all hairy, have tails, bark, and so on.

Concepts enable us to simplify our experience by organising our multitudinous perceptions under convenient headings. For Kirsch, concepts are central to human intelligence:

> There are many ways of thinking ... which clearly rely on concepts. Recall of cases, analogical reasoning, taking advice, posting reminders, thoughtful preparation, mental simulation, imagination, and second guessing are a few. I do not think that those mental activities are scarce, or confined to a fraction of our lives.

Source: Kirsch (1991)

And he insists that not only are concepts crucial in perception, learning and control, they are also – contrary to the assumptions of behaviour-based robotics – involved in the management of action. Imagine a robot in a situation where one of its goals (FOLLOW-WALL, for instance) comes into conflict with another (AVOID-OBSTACLE, say). In Brooks's behaviour-based approach, conflicts like this are resolved within the wiring of the subsumption architecture or by cues from the environment. However, Kirsch argues that if a robot is to cope with many competing goals, it is not clear that an action can be selected in so simple a fashion. He asks the following question:

> How is choice to be made? Prudent decision-making in such situations requires an all-things-considered approach. It requires balancing the recommendations, and setting a course of action which may involve the future coordination of a complex network of acts. It is hard to see how this could be done without the simplifications of the world which conceptualization gives us ... This adaptation of future expectations is impossible to explain without concepts ...

> When desire systems get large there must be some type of desire management, such as deliberation, weighing competing benefits and costs, and so on. This applies whether the [robot] is out there in the field doing my bidding or it is an autonomous creature with its own set of desires.

Source: Kirsch (1991)

Only when the environment gives a definite cue to a reactive robot as to what to do next will the robot be able to settle which course of action to take. Otherwise, it will need to represent alternative courses of action and then decide which might lead to dead ends, traps, loops or idle wandering. Any task that requires knowledge about the world from reasoning or recall, rather than by direct perception, Kirsch concludes, cannot be accomplished by a purely reactive agent.

Exercise 1.9

Try to think of some examples of tasks in which the environment cannot be relied on to give clear cues as to what to do next.

Discussion ....

The following tasks were identified by Kirsch:

▶ activities which involve other agents;

▶ activities which require response to events and actions beyond the agent's current perception, such as taking precautions now for the future, avoiding future dangers and idle wandering;

▶ activities which require understanding of a situation from an objective point of view, such as taking advice, following a new recipe or generalising from one context to another;

▶ activities which require problem solving;

▶ activities which are creative, such as musical performance, much of language use and self-amusement.

These are hardly isolated situations in a normal human life, but rather part of the fabric of human existence.

The requirement for concepts and internal representations is a clear challenge to biologically inspired AI. You may remember from Block 5, though, that many roboticists are well aware of this need and are taking first steps towards developing robots with emergent internal states.

The A-Life route to AI

The route map between sub-symbolic, reactive emergent systems and the abstract, symbolic complexities of human intelligence is one that has yet to be properly started. But most cognitive scientists do insist on the continuum view of nature, although the continuum may not be a straightforward one. According to Godfrey-Smith, for example, there are three ways in which life and mind can relate to each other in a continuum:

▶ *Weak continuity*. Anything that has a mind is alive, although not everything that is alive has a mind. Cognition is an activity of living systems.

▶ *Strong continuity*. Life and mind have a common abstract pattern or set of basic properties. The properties that are characteristic of mind are an enriched version of the fundamental properties of life in general. Mind is literally life-like.

▶ *Methodological continuity*. Understanding mind requires understanding the role it plays within entire living systems. Cognition should be investigated in the context of the whole organism.

The common theme here is that life and mind are entwined. Some cognitive scientists therefore claim that, in the same way that biological life seems to be the basis of natural intelligence, so *artificial life* should be the basis of artificial intelligence. In short, A-Life is a route – perhaps *the* route – to AI.

In 'Artificial life: a constructive lower bound for artificial intelligence', computer scientist Richard Belew argues that:

> Reasonable people can disagree about the phylogenetic distribution of natural intelligence: Are only people intelligent? Are primates? How about your dog or cat? Fish? Cockroaches? We might each be impressed by some different, particular intellectual skill and the species than can accomplish it, but one incontrovertible feature of all these examples of naturally occurring intelligence

Phylogeny refers to the development or evolution of a particular group of organisms.

is that they are alive. An A-Life approach to AI holds as a central tenet that this shared characteristic is not coincidental. The A-Life-AI claim is, 'The smartest dumb thing you can do is stay alive.' That is, A-Life represents a lower bound for AI. Further, the basic repertoire of abilities that let an organism stay alive are the building blocks with which we can try to build more impressive intelligences.

Source: Belew (1991)

SAQ 1.9

Where in this course have you come across an earlier 'building blocks' approach to AI? What were the problems with that approach and to what extent do you think they might apply to an A-Life approach to AI?

ANSWER..

You looked at the notion of a 'building blocks' approach to AI in connection with the construction of microworlds in Symbolic AI (such as Winograd's SHRDLU) in Block 2. The problem with this approach is that it does not scale. Microworlds are abstractions of the real world and the real world cannot practically be modelled by 'gluing' these microworld models together.

The A-Life approach shifts the building blocks from the environment to the behaviours of the agents embedded within it. In this way, A-Life practitioners hope that it may be possible to avoid the scaling problems associated with Symbolic AI. However, many A-Life systems use closed 'toy' environments too (think of the evolutionary robots in Block 5), so the problem of the microworld ghetto looms large here also. As Belew himself admits, 'there is an inherent contradiction between A-Life's simplified artificial environments and the richness of the natural world'. However, note that in a collection of interacting, evolving agents, the environment of each agent will itself be evolving and 'open', since that environment includes all the other evolving agents. Furthermore, as you saw in Block 3, many behaviour-based robotic systems do operate in the real world and hence are immune to this criticism.

Although many A-Life and AI practitioners believe that A-Life is, in some way, a precursor and basis for AI, not all agree. For example, computer scientist Aaron Sloman has argued that AI and A-Life are essentially different ways of studying the same thing. A-Life includes AI, because the processes studied in A-Life include the evolution of various kinds and degrees of intelligence. However, AI also includes A-Life, as AI researchers explore ways of including evolutionary mechanisms within problem-solving systems:

> Instead of arguing over whether the entities studied in A-Life, or in AI, are alive or conscious or intelligent, or worrying about where to draw the boundaries between those which REALLY are and those which are not, we can simply note that different more refined versions of our old indefinite concepts can be defined, with different boundaries.

Source: Sloman (1998)

If A-Life really is the route to AI, then does it offer an escape from the Chinese Room? I'll pay a last visit to that place.

Can A-Life help AI to escape the Chinese Room?

The Chinese Room Argument was designed to show that it was possible for a system to pass the Turing Test in the absence of genuine understanding and, therefore, intelligence, and so to demonstrate the impossibility of strong Symbolic AI. But given the claim that A-Life might be a route to AI, we have to consider whether the Chinese Room Argument applies here as well. But we need a new test first – a Turing Test for *life*.

Exercise 1.10

Spend the next few minutes thinking about what would be involved in constructing a Turing Test for life. Write down your answer. (Hint: You need to think about the type of participants in the test and the criteria used to establish a 'pass'.)

Discussion ....

Perhaps the simplest way to do this is to take the original Turing Test and substitute the human being and the computer (or candidate AI system) with a non-human biological life form and an A-Life form of some kind, respectively. The criteria by which the presence or otherwise of life in the two systems are to be judged would include those discussed in Unit 1 of Block 3.

Can the Chinese Room Argument be used against such a test? Although attempts have been made to extend Searle's original thought experiment to A-Life systems, a number of researchers in the field have contested their validity. For example, philosopher Brian Keeley has argued that the translation of AI concepts, metaphors and arguments into A-Life terms is invalid. Perhaps the most significant reason he gives is that life is a purely *objective*, third-person phenomenon: its presence or absence can, in principle, be firmly established by an outsider. Mind, or at least a conscious mind, is a *subjective*, first-person phenomenon: only the person who *has* the mind can know for sure that he or she has it. According to Keeley:

> One of the things that makes psychology such a difficult endeavour is that in addition to the straightforward *behavioural* third-person phenomena which stand in need of explanation, in the case of humans at least, there seem to be additional *experiential*, first-person phenomena.

Source: Keeley (1994)

If consciousness is vital to meaning and intelligence, then the Chinese Room Argument may apply to biologically inspired systems. Life itself is not a first-person phenomenon and so the thought experiment does not apply to it: first-person consciousness is not necessary for life. Keeley refers to 'the lack of anything analogous to the "problem of consciousness" in A-Life'. He rejects the claim that the philosophy of A-Life should be the philosophy of AI translated into biological terms.

The whole principle of A-Life as a route to AI is problematic for this reason. In the continuum view of nature, life and natural intelligence, somewhere along the line conscious, subjective, self-aware minds emerged from the objective, third-person interplay of atoms and molecules. Nobody has a clue when, where or how. How does one generate subjectivity from objectivity? Nobody knows. Until this problem is solved – if, indeed, it can be solved at all – it is questionable whether A-Life, or any kind of biologically inspired system, offers AI an exit from the Chinese Room. We may need to consider alternative escape strategies.

So this final question remains. I am intelligent (up to a point). Does the fact that I am intelligent have something to do with the fact that I am *conscious*? Is the fact that my perceptions and thoughts are intentional, have *meaning*, are *about* something, related in some way to my conscious awareness?

So far, I've hardly mentioned **consciousness**. But it is the gorilla skulking in the corner of every room in which intelligence – natural or artificial – is debated. Let's say a final few words about it now.

3.8 The gorilla in the room – intentionality, consciousness and AI

Conscious experience is something we all know about, but which is exceptionally hard to pin down in words. As David Chalmers puts it:

> ... there is something it feels like to be a cognitive agent. This internal aspect is conscious experience. Conscious experiences range from vivid colour sensations to experiences of the faintest background aromas; from hard edged pains to the elusive experience of thoughts on the tip of one's tongue; from mundane sounds and smells to the encompassing grandeur of musical experience; ... from the specificity of the taste of peppermint to the generality of one's experience of selfhood. All of these have a distinct experienced quality. All are prominent parts of the inner life of the mind.
>
> Source: Chalmers (1996)

Yet consciousness is ultimately mysterious:

> ... consciousness is surprising. If all we knew were the facts of physics, and even the facts about dynamics and information processing in complex systems, there would be no compelling reason to postulate the existence of conscious experience. If it were not for our direct evidence in the first-person case, the hypothesis would seem unwarranted; almost mystical, perhaps.
>
> Source: Chalmers (1996)

This problem has come to be known within scientific circles as the **hard problem** (of consciousness). It is this: how can *mind* – consciousness, first-personhood, subjective awareness, experiences, sensations, feelings and perceptions – in short, *what-it-is-like-to-be* something – arise from the *body*, something which is non-mental, material, objective, third-person, mechanical?

What is consciousness? Nobody knows (although you'll find there are plenty of opinions on the subject). How does it arise? Nobody knows. Perhaps the most serious problem for any form of strong AI lies in the phenomenon of consciousness and how to explain it. According to Brooks:

> As the complexity of the world increases, and the complexity of processing to deal with that world rises, we will see the same evidence of thought and consciousness in our systems as we see in people other than ourselves now. Thought and consciousness will not need to be programmed in. They will emerge.
>
> Source: Brooks (1991b)

And researchers in Symbolic AI have no clearer answer either. Either consciousness will somehow appear in a suitably complex artificial system, or it is of no relevance or importance anyway. But conscious experience seems central to mental life and so surely must be relevant to strong AI. There are good grounds for linking consciousness to intentionality and, therefore, to intelligence – at least *human* intelligence. Given the difficulty of constructing the route map from sub-symbolic natural intelligence to symbolic human intelligence, and the possible link between consciousness and human intelligence, thinkers such as Brooks might well have things the wrong way round: consciousness may not emerge from intelligence; rather, intelligence may emerge from consciousness.

4 Summary of Unit 1

In this unit, I've had two distinct aims: to hazard a guess about the future, and to take a last, critical look back at biologically inspired AI.

Most prophesies turn to be out tragically wrong. The human tendency is always to see the future as some kind of extension of the present. It seldom, if ever, is. So it's more than likely that my suggestions about the future of biologically inspired AI will turn out to be hopelessly off the mark. I have reviewed a number of lines of research that are currently active – in immune system computing, bio-inspired hardware, DNA computing, etc. It's quite probable that many of these may fizzle out in failure, as they hit insurmountable problems or as the winds of fashion that sweep across most computing (and every other) research areas change direction. A very few might become the basis of billion dollar industries and inaugurate new technological eras. We can only speculate.

Later in the unit I returned to the thorny question of intelligence, and whether we've succeeded in replicating it in machines. As you saw, the arguments about this sway back and forth, and are no nearer resolution than they were in the 1950s, when the question first arose. Many technologists are impatient with philosophical musings about the machines they build. They see their job as being to create effective solutions to practical problems. So it's important that we end on a positive note: nothing in Section 3 of this unit is an argument against *weak AI*. Strong AI may be within our grasp, or as far away as ever, or a complete impossibility. Whatever the truth of the matter, the technological enterprise of biologically inspired AI – producing practical systems that are only 'intelligent' in the weakest sense – will carry on, will continue to produce interesting and useful practical results, and will be supremely worth pursuing.

Now look back at the learning outcomes for this unit and check these against what you think you can now do. Return to any section of the unit if you need to.

Conclusion to Block 6

Block 6 conclusion

The end of Block 6 is also the end of M366. Our course really started with the figure of Alan Turing, the mathematical genius whose insights led to the computer, one of the most subtle and profound technologies humanity has devised; to a trillion dollar industry, employing millions; and to a new era in human communication and control. It's fitting that the course should end with him also.

An often neglected fact about Turing is that he was intensely interested in living systems, as were von Neumann, the cyberneticists and all the other founders of our field. Turing himself did pioneering work in embryology and the mathematics of morphogenesis. But, somewhere along the way, as the field of computing developed, the original biological insights and inspirations were lost.

In M366, the authors tried to trace their rediscovery. In Block 1, we contrasted Cybernetics and Symbolic AI, and described how the principles of Cybernetics went into eclipse after the 1950s. Essentially, M366 has been about how Cybernetics was reborn: in neural networks, in evolutionary computation, in reactive robots, and in the intelligence of swarms. Each of these, and others, are teeming research areas in their own right. We've often been able to offer you little more than an insight into them. To repeat a remark we made earlier, though, our best hope is that some of you may be motivated to enter one of them yourselves.

Finally, look back at the learning outcomes for this block and check these against what you think you can now do. Return to any section if you need to.

References and further reading

Further reading

Blackmore, S. (2006) *Conversations on Consciousness*, Oxford, Oxford University Press.

Forbes, N.S. (2004) *The Imitation of Life: How biology is inspiring computing*, Cambridge MA, MIT Press.

Sipper, M. (2002) *Machine Nature: The coming age of bio-inspired computing*, New York, McGraw-Hill Education.

References

Adler, M.J. (1990) *Intellect: Mind over matter*, New York, Collier Books.

Bedau, M.A. (1992) 'Philosophical aspects of artificial life', in Varela, F. and Bourgine, P. (eds) *Towards a Practice of Autonomous Systems*, Cambridge MA, MIT Press, pp. 494–503.

Bedau, M.A. and Packard, N.H. (1991) 'Measurement of evolutionary activity, teleology, and life', in Langton, C.G., Taylor, C., Farmer, J.D. and Rasmussen, S. (eds) *Artificial Life II*, Reading MA, Addison-Wesley, pp. 431–461.

Belew, R.K. (1991) 'Artificial life: a constructive lower bound for artificial intelligence', *IEEE Expert*, vol. 6, no. 1, pp. 8–15.

Bringsjord, S. and Noel, R. (2002) 'Real robots and the missing thought-experiment in the Chinese Room dialectic', in Preston, J. and Bishop, M. (eds) *Views into the Chinese Room: New essays on Searle and artificial intelligence*, Oxford, Clarendon Press, pp. 144–166.

Brooks, R.A. (1987) 'Elephants don't play chess', *Robotics and Autonomous Systems*, vol. 6, pp. 3–15.

Brooks, R.A. (1991a) 'Intelligence without representation', *Artificial Intelligence*, vol. 47, pp. 139–159.

Brooks, R.A. (1991b) 'Intelligence without reason', in Mylopoulos, J. and Reiter, R. (eds) *Proceedings of 12th International Joint Conference on Artificial Intelligence*, Sydney, Australia, Morgan Kaufmann, pp. 569–595.

Brooks, R.A. (1997) 'From earwigs to humans', *Robotics and Autonomous Systems*, vol. 20, nos. 2–4, pp. 291–304.

Brooks, R.A. (2001) 'The relationship between matter and life', *Nature*, vol. 409, pp. 409–411.

Chalmers, D.J. (1992) 'Subsymbolic computation and the Chinese Room', in Dinsmore, J. (ed.) *The Symbolic and Connectionist Paradigms: Closing the gap*, Hillsdale NJ, Lawrence Erlbaum Associates, pp. 25–48.

Chalmers, D.J. (1996) *The Conscious Mind*, Oxford, Oxford University Press.

Chrisley, R. (2003) 'Embodied artificial intelligence', *Artificial Intelligence*, vol. 149, pp. 131–150.

Clynes, M. and Kline, N. (1961) 'Psychophysiological aspects of space flight', in Flaherty, B.E. (ed.) *Drugs, Space and Cybernetics: Evolution to cyborgs*, New York, Columbia University Press, pp. 355–371.

Collins, H.M. (1996) 'Embedded or embodied? A review of Hubert Dreyfus', *What Computers* Still *Can't Do, Artificial Intelligence*, vol. 80, pp. 99–117.

Collins, H.M. (2000) 'Four kinds of knowledge, two (or maybe three) kinds of embodiment, and the question of artificial intelligence', in Wrathall, M.A. and Malpas, J. (eds) *Heidegger, Coping, and Cognitive Science: Essays in honor of Hubert L. Dreyfus, Volume 2*, Cambridge MA, MIT Press, pp. 179–195.

Dennett, D.C. (1987) *The Intentional Stance*, Cambridge MA, MIT Press.

Dreyfus, H.L. (1993) *What Computers Still Can't Do: A critique of artificial reason*, Cambridge MA, MIT Press.

Godfrey-Smith, P. (1994) 'Spencer and Dewey on life and mind', in Brooks, R.A. and Maes, P. (eds) *Artificial IV*, Cambridge MA, MIT Press, pp. 80–89.

Harnad, S. (1990) 'The symbol grounding problem', *Physica D*, vol. 42, pp. 335–346.

Harnad, S. (1995) 'Grounding symbolic capacity in robotic capacity', in Steels, L. and Brooks, R. (eds) *The Artificial Life Route to Artificial Intelligence: Building embodied, situated agents*, Hillsdale NJ, Lawrence Erlbaum Associates, pp. 277–286.

Keeley, B.L. (1994) 'Against the global replacement: on the application of the philosophy of artificial intelligence to artificial life', in Langton, C.G. (ed.) *Artificial Life III: SFI Studies in the sciences of complexity*, Redwood City CA, Addison-Wesley, pp. 569–587.

Kirsch, D. (1991) 'Today the earwig, tomorrow man?', *Artificial Intelligence*, vol. 47, pp. 161–184.

Langton, C.G. (1989) 'Artificial life', in Langton, C.G. (ed.) *Artificial Life: Proceedings of the first workshop on the synthesis and simulation of living systems*, Reading MA, Addison-Wesley, pp. 1–47.

Lanier, J. (1995) 'Agents of alienation', *Interactions*, vol. 2, no. 3, pp. 66–72.

Preston, J. and Bishop, M. (eds) (2002) *Views into the Chinese Room: New essays on Searle and artificial intelligence*, Oxford, Clarendon Press.

Searle, J.R. (1980) 'Minds, brains, and programs', *Behavioural and Brain Sciences*, vol. 3, pp. 417–424.

Searle, J.R. (1990) 'Is the brain's mind a computer program?', *Scientific American*, vol. 262, no. 1, pp. 20–25.

Searle, J.R. (1992) *The Rediscovery of the Mind*, Cambridge MA, MIT Press.

Sloman, A. (1998) 'AI and A-Life: Notes in response to a journalist's request for an overview', http://www.cs.bham.ac.uk/~axs/misc/alife.and.ai.txt (accessed 18 May 2007).

Smith, B.C. (1999) 'Situatedness/embeddedness', in Wilson, R.A. and Keil, F.C. (eds) *The MIT Encyclopedia of the Cognitive Sciences*, Cambridge MA, MIT Press, pp. 769–771.

Whitby, B. (1997) 'Why the Turing Test is AI's biggest blind alley', in Millican, P. and Clark, A. (eds) *Machines and Thought: The legacy of Alan Turing, Volume 1*, Oxford, Clarendon Press, pp. 53–63.

Acknowledgements

Grateful acknowledgement is made to the following sources for permission to reproduce material within this course text.

Text

Searle, J. R. (1980) 'Minds brains and programs', *Behavioral and Brain Sciences*, vol. 3, no. 3. Copyright © 1980 Cambridge University Press. Reproduced by permission.

Figures

Figure 1.1(a): Copyright © 1996–2005 by Jesse Prinz;

Figure 1.1(b): Copyright © Jolyon Troscianko 2003.

Cover image

Image used on the cover and elsewhere: Daniel H. Janzen.

Index for Block 6